How Do I Forgive?

by

Pamela Harrison

How Do I Forgive?
by Pamela Harrison

ISBN: 978-0-9885426-0-0

Printed in the United States of America.

Contents

Did you know that forgiveness comes in levels?
Depending on where you are individually, you will
more than likely find yourself in one of these categories:
First: "I don't want to forgive… I need God to give me
the desire to forgive."
Second: "I desperately desire to forgive; I just can't seem
to bring myself to completely forgive."
Third: "I thought I had forgiven, but every time I
see (name here), I'm flooded with the memories of
what they did to me and overwhelmed with negative
emotions."

What does it really mean to forgive? To "forgive" means,
"to cease to feel resentment against (an offender)."

Ah! But how do we get to the place that we are able to
cease to feel anger towards those who wrong us?

There are two key elements in being able to forgive:

• Being able to receive forgiveness from God
• Choosing to forgive ourselves

FACT: When we freely receive forgiveness, we will
freely forgive.

A Story about Forgiveness

Here's a good example to get us started:

> *Matthew 18:21-35 (MSG)*
> *21 At that point Peter got up the nerve to ask,*
> *"Master, how many times do I forgive a brother or*
> *sister who hurts me? Seven?"*
> *22 Jesus replied, "Seven! Hardly. Try seventy times*
> *seven."*

23-25 "The kingdom of God is like a king who decided to square accounts with his servants. As he got under way, one servant was brought before him who had run up a debt of a hundred thousand dollars. He couldn't pay up, so the king ordered the man, along with his wife, children, and goods, to be auctioned off at the slave market."

Side Note: Imagine if here in the US, you had to go before the president each year to pay off the debt you acquired throughout the previous year. At that time you would be expected to pay the debt in full or the president would order your home to be sold, your cars to be sold – everything you owned –to be sold off. Not only that, but then you and every immediate family member would be placed on a farm here in the US to work until the debt was paid off.

Now think about what would happen once the debt was paid in full and you were released. How would you buy a home? Where would you go live? How would you even buy a tent to live in while you're looking for a job in order to be able to build your life back? We may find that we would respond exactly as this man. Let's find out what he did and what the king decided to do:

26-27 "The poor wretch threw himself at the king's feet and begged, 'Give me a chance and I'll pay it all back.' Touched by his plea, the king let him off, erasing the (entire $100,000.00) debt."
28 "The servant was no sooner out of the room when he came upon one of his fellow servants who owed him ten dollars ($10 whole bucks!). He

*seized him by the throat and demanded, 'Pay up.
Now!'*
*29-31 "The poor wretch threw himself down and
begged, 'Give me a chance and I'll pay it all back.'
But he wouldn't do it. He had him arrested and
put in jail until the debt was paid. When the other
servants saw this going on, they were outraged and
brought a detailed report to the king.*
*32-35 "The king summoned the man and said,
'You evil servant! I forgave your entire debt
when you begged me for mercy. Shouldn't you be
compelled to be merciful to your fellow servant who
asked for mercy?' The king was furious and put
the screws to the man until he paid back his entire
debt. And that's exactly what my Father in heaven
is going to do to each one of you who doesn't forgive
unconditionally anyone who asks for mercy."*

Important: Matthew 6:15 and 18:35 state that we must
forgive before we can be forgiven. However, what is
often forgotten and not explained, and has led many to
believe the Bible is full of contradictions, is that while
Jesus walked the earth, the Jews were still under the
Law, what we call today the Old Covenant.

The Law was put in place to show each person what
was sinful and what was expected of man in order to
put himself in right standing before God. This is the
summation of the Law: The Law was put in place to
show man he is a sinner in need of a Savior.

**These verses were spoken by Jesus before He shed
His blood, cutting a New Covenant and putting**

us under grace. Because we are under God's grace, thanks to Jesus, we are now freely and completely forgiven.

Now, under the New Covenant of grace, as a result of simple belief in Jesus being the atoning sacrifice for all sin of all mankind, we are completely and freely forgiven—just like the man from our example in Matthew 18.

In Luke 17:1, Jesus said, *"It is impossible for the stumbling blocks (offenses) not to come."* We are going to be offended and we are going to be wronged.

However, we have a choice. We can choose to be mindful and grateful that the large debt of all our wrongdoing—all our sins, past, present, and future – have been punished in the body of Jesus and we are debt free before God forever. We can know that our account has been wiped clean because of Jesus paying the price for every sin. Or we can choose to be like the poor wretch in our example and quickly forget how large of a debt we owed and how close we came to losing everything if not for the mercy of our King. The choice is ours. Which will you choose?

The more freely we receive the forgiveness that is already ours, the more we will freely forgive ourselves and others. When we receive the truth that we are freely and completely forgiven, the result will be that we freely forgive others.

However, we must stay mindful of the FACT that only because of Jesus are we in right standing before God.

When we know that we have blown it, or when some-one offends us (or a loved one – a borrowed offense), we have a choice to make.

When we receive forgiveness, we refuse to be unforgiving with others because we understand that God freely forgives us. The assurance of God's forgiveness in our lives is that Jesus was the sacrifice for all sin, which causes us to stay in right standing with God—no matter what. This is grace!

You may say, "I'm not yet convinced that I'm freely and completely forgiven." That's okay! Next, we are going to see scriptures that teach us that we are forgiven – only because of Jesus' sacrifice. These scriptures are the foundation to us becoming rooted in righteousness:

> *Hebrews 10:11-18 (MSG)*
> *11-18 ...Christ made a single sacrifice for sins, and that was it!.... It was a perfect sacrifice by a perfect person to perfect some very imperfect people. By that single offering, he did everything that needed to be done for everyone who takes part in the purifying process.... (The purifying process: receiving Jesus as our Savior; understanding that His sacrifice was the payment needed for sin, a blood sacrifice – a "once and for all" blood sacrifice.) He concludes, I'll forever wipe the slate clean of their sins. Once sins are taken care of for good, there's no longer any need to offer sacrifices for them.*
> *Romans 4:25 (NIV)*
> *25 He was delivered over to death for our sins and was raised to life for our justification."*

Romans 5:18-19 (MSG)
18-19 Here it is in a nutshell: Just as one person did it wrong and got us in all this trouble with sin and death, another person did it right and got us out of it. But more than just getting us out of trouble, he got us into life! One man said no to God and put many people in the wrong; one man said yes to God and put many in the right.

Hebrews 10:10 (NIV)
10 We have been made holy through the sacrifice of the body of Jesus Christ once for all.

Romans 3:23- 25 (NIV)
23 For all have sinned and fall short of the glory of God, 24 and are justified freely by his grace through the redemption that came by Christ Jesus. 25 God presented him as a sacrifice of atonement, through faith in his blood.

In order to be able to forgive – whether it is someone that wronged us, who does not intend to admit it or ask our forgiveness, or it is someone who has admitted wronging us, but we find it difficult to forgive them – we must first do one thing as believers. We must receive the forgiveness that is already ours!

The more we are rooted in righteousness, (meaning, the more we understand that we are freely forgiven), the more freely we will be able to forgive. We must understand our righteousness is only because of Jesus and that we never lose our right standing before God, no matter what. This enables us to freely forgive others!

You may be thinking, "I thought I had forgiven, but each time a memory flashes in my mind, I feel so angry!"

Many of us know the saying, "I may forgive, but I will never forget!" So let's address this saying, because for many of you reading this, it rings true.

Knowing we're both spirit and soul, it's important to understand what makes up the soul. Our soul is our mind, will, and emotions. When we have a thought or memory, it provokes an emotion and our will always follows our emotions. Similarly, negative thoughts or memories provoke negative emotions.

"But I will never forget what was done to me," we may say.

We are not required to forget the wrong done. But for our benefit, for us to be able to move on and enjoy life, we must forgive. So when the memory crosses our mind and the negative emotions kick in, we are at a POINT OF DECISION at that very moment: "Am I going with my feelings or am I going to push through and override the feelings I'm having?"

Important Fact: Emotions are not fact.

Emotions are powerful. They are compelling and convincing, but they are not fact. When we are led by our emotions, we are unstable, and will experience self-sabotaging behavior.

"But how do I make my feelings change? How do I make my negative feelings go away?"

Answer: We must choose to push through to override what we are feeling, and say out of our mouths in that moment:

"No, I have chosen to forgive just as I am already forgiven by God! Devil, I ain't buying what you're selling. I have chosen to forgive (name here) and I refuse to be fooled by you or buy back into unforgiveness. I refuse to dwell on these memories."

Beware! You have an enemy who desires to steal your divine destiny!

What we must never forget about the enemy of our soul, Satan, is that his only inroad into our lives is through our thoughts. Because of the sacrifice of Jesus, the finished work of the cross, Jesus stripped the enemy of his power (Colossians 2:15).

Sin in our life does not give the enemy an inroad or the right to come steal from us. No. Now that we are under grace, his only inroad into our lives is through our thoughts. The enemy comes to steal the word from our mind, from our hearts, and to plant his thoughts (Matthew 13:19).

We have protection!

> *Ephesians 6:11-17 (NIV)*
> *11 Put on the full armor of God, so that you can take your stand against the devil's schemes. 12 For our struggle is not against flesh and blood, but against the rulers, against the authorities, against the powers of this dark world and against the spiritual forces of evil in the heavenly realms.*

*13 Therefore put on the full armor of God, so
that when the day of evil comes, you may be able
to stand your ground, and after you have done
everything, to stand. 14 Stand firm then, with **the
belt of truth** buckled around your waist...*

What is the truth? Jesus took all the punishment
for all your sins, you are completely forgiven,
and you have been given the gift of permanent
righteous before God.

*... with the **breastplate of righteousness** in place...*

What is the breastplate? It is a piece of plate
armor partially or completely covering the front
of the torso protecting one's heart and lungs –
our physical life source. Knowing we have been
made right before God as a result of our faith
(belief) in Jesus having made us right is our
spiritual breastplate, protecting our spiritual life
source.

*15 ... and with your feet fitted with the readiness
that comes from the **gospel of peace**.*

What is the "gospel of peace"? The good news
of Jesus taking the punishment for all our sins,
thus making peace between God and man and
bringing peace and rest to as many as will believe.

*16 In addition to all this, take up the **shield of
faith**, with which you can extinguish all the
flaming arrows of the evil one.*

What is the "shield of faith"? <u>Faith is belief in
Jesus having taken the punishment for all our</u>

sins, once for all. Faith enables us to receive the gift of no condemnation. Once believed and received, the believer is empowered to withstand any "flaming arrows," – any attempt to pull us out of the peace that we are completely forgiven, unconditionally loved, and accepted as sons or daughters of God Himself. This brings the believer to the place where he or she can stand firm and say with complete confidence: "I may have messed up, but because of grace, because of Jesus taking the punishment due me, God will not punish me. He will not withhold any good thing. I am right before God as a gift!

17 Take the **helmet of salvation...**

The helmet of salvation is the gear needed to protect our minds, the only inroad of the enemy.

... and **the sword of the Spirit, whic**h **is the word of God.**

The Word of God is what Jesus did for us and who we are now as a result.

An example of lifting the shield of faith is when we insist on believing the Word of God and become one who defiantly opposes the enemy.

If hit with the thought you have not forgiven, you can say with great conviction: "I am freely and completely forgiven, according to Romans 3:23,24. Therefore, I choose to freely forgive (name here), and I refuse to be moved by my emotions!"

It is only when we think on the thoughts the enemy shoots into our minds, the "flaming arrows," that we see the enemy gain victory in our lives. It's when we choose to believe and think on God's words, making the Word of God the final authority in our life, that we walk in the victory that is already ours.

2 Corinthians 10:4, 5 (YLT)
*4 "... for the weapons of our warfare [are] not fleshly, but powerful to God for bringing down of strongholds, 5 ... and every high thing lifted up against the knowledge of God, and **bringing into captivity every thought to the obedience of the Christ...**"*

Food for thought: What is "the obedience of Christ"?

Christ obeyed the will of God for His life, laid down His life for us, took the punishment due us, and died the death we deserved, all so that we would be completely free before God and free from the strongholds of the enemy. Each time we face a challenge or the testing of our faith, we must choose to "take captive every thought" that is contrary to what Christ did, who we are, and what we now have as a result of what Jesus did for us.

Important: These challenges and tests of our faith are not necessarily sent by God, but come simply as a result of us living in a fallen world.

Who are we now? We are holy, righteous, and perfect before God because of what Jesus did for us. He became our substitute in a beautiful exchange that took place on the cross, when He who knew no sin became sin for us (2 Corinthians 5:21).

He not only took on our sin, but all weakness, sickness, and disease. He took care of it all on the cross and then He rose from the grave: strong, healthy, and wealthy.

First John 4:17 says, *"… as He (Jesus) is so are we in this world."*

Is Jesus weak or sick? Neither are you!
Is Jesus in lack? Neither are you!
Is He holy and righteous? So are you!

This is the good news! This is what Jesus did, who you really are, and what is rightfully yours!

Did you know that Love = Forgiveness?

John 3:16 says that God so loved the world (you and me) that He sent His Son not to condemn us (pronounce us guilty and unfit for use), but to SAVE us.

> *Colossians 3:12-14 (NIV)*
> *12 Therefore, as God's chosen people, holy and dearly loved, clothe yourselves with compassion, kindness, humility, gentleness and patience.*
> *13 Bear with each other and forgive whatever grievances you may have against one another. Forgive as the Lord forgave you. 14 And over all these virtues put on love, which binds them all together in perfect unity.*

> *Ephesians 4:31-32 (NIV)*
> *31 Get rid of all bitterness, rage and anger, brawling and slander, along with every form of malice. 32 Be kind and compassionate to one another, forgiving each other, just as in Christ God forgave you.*

Many want to know: "How do I become so full of love that I am able to love others, even the unlovable?"

Answer: Time in the presence of Love... God who is Love (1 John 4)!

When we choose to receive His love, His forgiveness, and just as important – forgive ourselves – we will give out what we are full of = Love and Forgiveness!
You may say: "I don't feel loved by God. I don't feel worthy of God's love. I feel shame. I feel guilt. I feel unacceptable."

Remember, feelings are just that – they are not fact. We must insist on believing God's Word that tells us we are loved, we have been made worthy, and that sin never breaks our fellowship with God. When we do not believe that we are completely and freely forgiven, it causes us to push God away from us. It is when we believe our feelings over truth that we decide to pull away from God. Since He is our very source for change, when we pull away from Him it hinders our effortless transformation and only hope to become able to truly love and forgive others.

The Royal Law - The Law of Love

James 2:8,11-13 (NIV)
8 If you really keep the royal law found in Scripture, "Love your neighbor as yourself," you are doing right.
11 For he who said, "Do not commit adultery," also said, "Do not murder." If you do not commit adultery but do commit murder, you have become

a lawbreaker. 12 Speak and act as those who are going to be judged by the law (principle) that gives freedom, 13 because judgment without mercy will be shown to anyone who has not been merciful. Mercy triumphs over judgment!

What James is saying here is that if we will choose to love one another, we will not commit adultery, we will not murder, but will in essence keep the Law (God's holy moral standard). We will do so neither out of fear of judgment, nor out of fear of not having God's blessing, but simply to do right to others out of love, the right motive. We will obey the royal law effortlessly because we have chosen to spend time with God, who is love. In turn, we will give love, resulting in us fulfilling the royal law, the law of love.

The ability to forgive summed up:

When we are fully aware of how much we are loved and forgiven, we will walk in love and forgiveness.

What does it mean to "walk in love"?

Answer: To walk in love is to exhibit the attributes of love described in 1 Corinthians 13 every day as we encounter challenging people and situations. Too many try to love others within their own power. Human love can only take so much, last so long, and go so far. However, when we believe and receive the love of God, and make God our number one source for love, we will in turn give out what we are full of… love. The same is true of forgiveness. Knowing you are loved and knowing you are forgiven are key to loving and forgiving yourself and others. Knowing God loves you and has forgiven you work hand in hand. We must know we are loved to believe we are forgiven. We must know we are forgiven to believe we are loved.

These are the attributes of walking in love:

> *1 Corinthians 13:4-8a (NIV)*
> *4 Love is patient, love is kind. It does not envy, it does not boast, it is not proud. 5 It is not rude, it is not self-seeking, it is not easily angered, it keeps no record of wrongs. 6 Love does not delight in evil but rejoices with the truth. 7 It always protects, always trusts, always hopes, always perseveres. 8 Love never fails.*

Encouragement: Choose to believe you are righteous, knowing that righteousness is not found in your actions, but a person – Jesus. Jesus is our righteousness.

- Choose to become rooted in righteousness.
- Spend time acknowledging God's presence in you, with you, and for you; allow Him to love on you.
- Receive the forgiveness that is already yours and insist on forgiving yourself.

Important: Never allow any "feeling" to keep you from getting into the presence of God, no matter what. This is the enemy's trick to pull you away from the very connection that empowers you to do the will of God, be in the will of God, and stay in the will of God. This ability comes from being connected with God on a daily basis.

Romans 8:1 (NIV)
"Therefore there is now no condemnation for those who are in Christ Jesus."

The Message version of the Bible says it like this:

Romans 8:1-8 (MSG)
1-2 With the arrival of Jesus, the Messiah, that fateful dilemma is resolved. Those who enter into Christ's being-here-for-us no longer have to live under a continuous, low-lying black cloud. A new power is in operation. The Spirit of life in Christ, like a strong wind, has magnificently cleared the air, freeing you from a fated lifetime of brutal tyranny at the hands of sin and death.

3-4 God went for the jugular when he sent his own Son. He didn't deal with the problem as something remote and unimportant. In his Son, Jesus, he personally took on the human condition, entered the disordered mess of struggling humanity in order to set it right once and for all. The law code (requirements to follow the Ten Commandments under the Old Covenant), weakened as it always was by fractured human nature, could never have done that.

The law always ended up being used as a Band-Aid on sin instead of a deep healing of it. And now what the law code asked for but we couldn't deliver is accomplished as we, instead of redoubling our own efforts, simply embrace what the Spirit is doing in us.

*5-8 Those who think they can do it on their own
end up obsessed with measuring their own moral
muscle but never get around to exercising it in real
life. Those who trust God's action in them find
that God's Spirit is in them—living and breathing
God! Obsession with self in these matters is a dead
end; attention to God leads us out into the open,
into a spacious, free life. Focusing on the self is the
opposite of focusing on God. Anyone completely
absorbed in self ignores God, ends up thinking
more about self than God. That person ignores who
God is and what he is doing. And God isn't pleased
at being ignored.*

Simply put: Refuse to be sin-conscious. Be conscious
only of the gift of righteousness given to you because
of believing that Jesus paid the price for all your sins.
When you believe you are righteous, you will live righ-
teously – effortlessly!

You are loved. You are accepted. You are forgiven by
God.

Believe it - Receive it - Live it!

About the Author

 Pamela Harrison is a minister of the New Covenant. She passionately teaches others how to develop a personal and close relationship with God, and become rooted in righteousness – enabling them to overcome all of life's adversities!

Her commission is to make Jesus known to those that have not heard what He has done for them, as well as those hurt by, in bondage to, and blinded by "religion."

Because of the relationship Pamela has developed with her Savior Jesus, and the revelation of His grace, she has received healing and restoration from a childhood of abuse and life of dysfunction. God has used her to impart healing to those who are broken and bring restoration to those who desire to overcome life's adversities.

Her heart's desire is to see people saved, teach others how to develop a real and intimate relationship with Jesus by becoming rooted in righteousness, and to see His people healed and totally set free! She is passionate about seeing others fulfill their God-given destiny!

Pamela Harrison is a licensed and ordained minister of the Gospel. She has been ministering in the United States and third world countries as led by the Spirit of God to "go," as the passion for souls and to see people set free and healed is her mission.

Matt and Pamela Harrison live in the Tulsa area of Oklahoma. They have two beautiful adult children: Aliesha and Christian.

Salvation

If you would like to receive all that Jesus has supplied for you by making Him the Lord of your life, simply pray:

"Lord Jesus, thank you for loving me just as I am – and so much so that you died for me. I believe your innocent blood has washed me clean of every sin; past, present, and future. I believe that you died the death due me and that you rose from the grave, proving you are the Son of God, and justifying me before God. Because of you, I am now right before God permanently. No longer am I a sinner. Now I am a son/ daughter of God, sanctified (holy), permanently righteous before God. This righteousness was given to me as a gift from God – not something I could ever earn. It was given to me as a gift of God as a result of my belief in you, Jesus, the Son of God.

Jesus, I believe you are Lord, my Savior, now and forever. I thank you that never again will there be a hindrance between God and I because you have removed the only hindrances – sin – by taking the punishment for all sin, once and for all. Thank you for all you have done for me!

Thank you for filling me with your love, peace, and joy. Because you overcame – I know that I, too, can overcome!

In your name, Jesus – Amen!"

Pamela's Testimony

Pamela Harrison is a survivor and overcomer of childhood abuse, as well as rejection and abandonment even into her adult years.

After leaving home at age seventeen, she married at age nineteen, had her first child at nineteen, divorced at twenty-one, and married for the second time at the age of twenty-one.

When she was twenty-two, she had her second child. It was at that time, after she brought home her second child, that she had the thought: "*I am on my second marriage, and my second child and I'm only twenty-two years old. What am I going to do with my life?*"

From that time on, Pamela had the desire to be healed from the all the pain. She realized that because of the pain and unforgiveness within her, she was simply existing and not really living life with purpose.

For the next nine years, she experienced spiritual abuse. This is one of the most painful and devastating experiences one can have and many have yet to recover from it. In her writings and teachings, those who have suffered spiritual abuse will find that they can recover, become stronger, and grow wiser as a result!

After a childhood of abuse, nine years of spiritual abuse, and a series of devastating circumstances, she gave up. She was angry with God and man and decided she would take care of herself – that she needed NO ONE! She was full of anger, rage, unforgiveness, and skepticism.

This is when she started drinking and became an alcoholic for five of the most miserable years of her life.

Pamela's deliverance was not an overnight process, but instead a walking through and out process with the Holy Spirit. She has much to offer people, teaching them what the Word of God has to offer, walking them through the winds of contradiction (and challenge), and ministering with an anointing that destroys the yoke of bondage.

CPSIA information can be obtained
at www.ICGtesting.com
Printed in the USA
LVHW082156241019
635296LV00018B/828/P